UP CLOSE

Giant Dinosaurs

PAUL HARRISON

W

FRANKLIN WATTS
LONDON • SYDNEY

Published in 2009 by Franklin Watts
Reprinted in 2010

Copyright © 2009 Arcturus Publishing Limited

Franklin Watts
338 Euston Road
London NW1 3BH

Franklin Watts Australia
Level 17/207 Kent Street
Sydney, NSW 2000

Author: Paul Harrison
Editor Fiona Tulloch
Designers: Trevor Cook, Sally Henry

Picture credits: Bill Stoneham: 4 top, 16 bottom, 21 bottom; Corbis: 6 top, 11 bottom, 14 top, 17 top, 15 bottom, 19 bottom; DEA Picture Library: 15 top; Getty: 2, 7 bottom, Jon Hughes/Pixelshack: front cover, title page, 9 bottom, 11 top, 12 bottom, 13 top, 16 top, 18 bottom, 21 top, 22; Natural History Museum: 13 bottom, 14 bottom; Photoshot: 4 bottom, 5 bottom, 7 top, 8 bottom, 10 bottom, 18 top, 19 top, 20 top; Reuters: 10; Science Photo Library: 5, 20 bottom.

A CIP catalogue record for this book is available from the British Library

Dewey number: 567.9

ISBN: 978-1-4451-0170-5
SL000954EN

Printed in China

Franklin Watts is a division of Hachette Children's Books, an Hachette UK Company
www.hachette.co.uk

Contents

Kingdom of the Giants

What is it about *dinosaurs* that we find so fascinating? It's probably their size. Some of them were simply the biggest animals ever to walk the Earth.

KINGS OF THE WORLD

Dinosaurs dominated the planet for over 130 million years until they died out around 65 million years ago.

BIG IS BRILLIANT?

Being big and strong meant giant dinosaurs were relatively safe from attack. But they needed giant meals. If food was scarce, they could easily starve.

LAND SPREAD

Around 250 million years ago, there was only one land mass on the Earth. Slowly, this broke up to make the continents we have today. As a result, remains of giant dinosaurs are found all over the world.

It was once thought that having nostrils on the top of the head meant dinosaurs lived underwater.

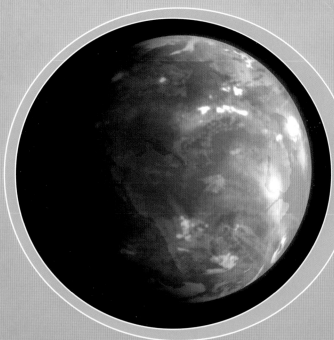

HIP HOORAY

All dinosaurs were *reptiles*, but dinosaurs had their legs underneath, rather than at the sides like modern reptiles. The shape of the hip bones helps to show the connection between dinosaurs and their descendents, the birds.

Meat Eaters

The dinosaur world had its fair share of huge *carnivores* and most of the plant eaters out there were easy prey for them.

AFRICAN GIANT

The Carcharodontosaurus was one of the biggest carnivores in North Africa during the Cretaceous period. At around 14 metres in length, it was even longer than Tyrannosaurus rex.

SMILE, PLEASE

Carcharodontosaurus means shark-toothed lizard. This 2-metre long skull, full of very sharp teeth, must have terrified the plant eaters of its day.

SCARY SOUTHERNER

Giganotosaurus has only recently been discovered in Argentina. It roamed South America in the middle Cretaceous period long before Tyrannosaurus rex arrived to terrorise North America.

HAIL TO THE KING!

Tyrannosaurus rex is possibly the most famous of all giant dinosaur species. Around 6 metres high, this massive meat eater was taller than a double-decker bus and had teeth as long as bananas. It could run as fast as a human being. Just as well they're not around today, then!

SIMPLY MASSIVE

Spinosaurus was possibly the biggest dinosaur carnivore ever found. Its remains were discovered in Egypt nearly a hundred years ago. It had a huge sail-like structure on its back and weighed up to 20 tonnes!

LEADER OF THE PACK

Allosaurus lived in North America during the Jurassic period. At 5 metres tall, it was not the biggest of dinosaurs. By hunting in packs, it could bring down the biggest plant eaters.

There were nearly twice as many plant-eating dinosaurs as meat-eating ones.

Huge Herbivores

During the Jurassic and Cretaceous periods, the great *herbivores* roamed the land in herds.

PLATE PUZZLER

Stegosaurus was huge and weighed up to 7 tonnes, but it wasn't very quick. It defended itself with a strong tail, which had 1-metre long spikes on it. The big plates on its back may have helped it control body temperature but nobody really knows for certain.

STRAIGHT TO THE POINT

Unlike the present-day rhinocerus, the Triceratops probably didn't charge at its enemies. Its horns were only strong enough to be used as prodding weapons.

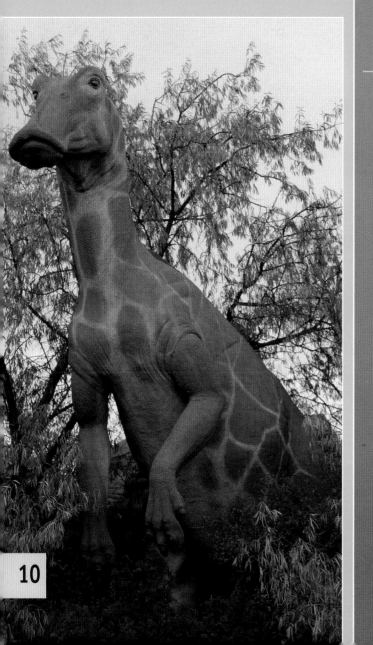

HADROSAUR IN A HURRY

Edmontosaurus belonged to the hadrosaur family of dinosaurs. It lived in large herds in North America during the Cretaceous period. Over 13 metres long and weighing around 3 tonnes, Edmontosaurus could run at the speed of a horse – handy for getting away from a hungry meat-eater.

HEAD CASE

Pachycephalosaurus lived in North America during the Cretaceous period. Once it was thought its strange dome-shaped head was used for defence. It's since been proved too weak for this, so its purpose remains a mystery.

THE COMPLETE FOSSIL

For many years, Brachiosaurus was the largest dinosaur known. In terms of complete *fossil* skeletons, it's still the biggest!

Soaring Sauropods

Sauropods were the biggest animals of the Mesozoic era. They lived in herds and fed on huge quantities of vegetation.

LOOKING DOWN

Diplodocus had short front legs making its head point downwards. This helped it eat plants which grew low down on the ground, such as ferns.

Many plant-eating dinosaurs swallowed small rocks to help them digest their food.

ARMOUR PLATED

At only 12 metres in length, the Saltasaurus was prey to the larger carnivores. Its defence was a covering of small bony plates that acted as a kind of armour.

FUSSY EATER

Brachytrachelopan had an unusually short neck for a *sauropod*. The neck bones were joined together, limiting the movement of its head. It fed on vegetation between 1 and 2 metres above the ground.

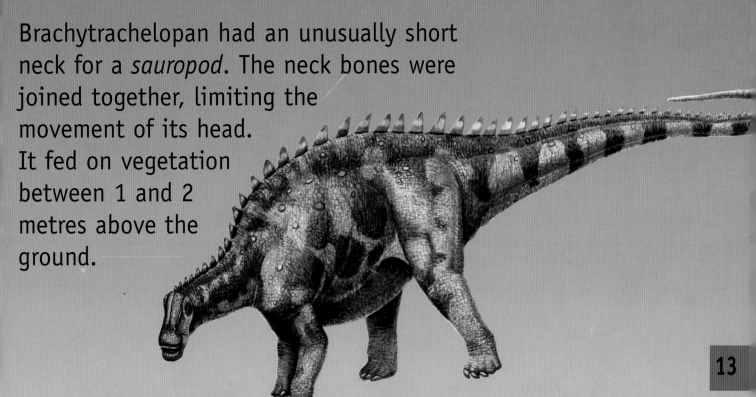

MISTAKEN IDENTITY

It seemed to be a new species, but the 25-metre long Brontosaurus was found to be an Apatosaurus.

SOME NECK

Sauropods were well known for their long neck. Mamenchisaurus had the longest – nearly half of its 11-metre length. It could reach high into the trees, but a sore throat must have been awful!

Flying High

As dinosaurs stalked the earth, flying reptiles soared overhead.

BIGGEST EVER?

Quetzalcoatlus was the largest flying animal ever. It's wingspan was about 11 metres – the size of a four-seater aircraft!

FLAP OR GLIDE?

An American scientist made a full-sized, remote control, flying model of Quetzalcoatlus. He proved that the animal used its wings like a bird.

CLAMMING UP

Dsungaripterus had a beak that was made for prising clams apart. The flat teeth at the back of its beak could have been used for crushing the shells.

Although they flew, pterosaurs did not evolve into birds — the dinosaurs did.

BAT BIRD

Pteranodon used its huge beak to scoop fish out of the water. The crest on its head may have been used to help steering, like the tail fin on an airplane.

LIGHTWEIGHT

Ornithocheirus had a giant wingspan like Quetzalcoatlus. In spite of its size, it was very light. It had hollow bones which were very strong for their weight.

OLD DEVIL

Anhanguera (meaning 'old devil') was a giant fish-eating *pterosaur* which lived in the Cretaceous period in Brazil. Its discovery helped to solve the question of whether pterosaurs walked on two legs or four.

Superstars of the Sea

During the Mesozoic era, the sea was full of giant-sized carnivores.

OVER-INFLATED

Liopleurodon was a ferocious *predator*. Its 3-metre-long skull was full of sharp teeth.

PLESIOSAUR PREDATOR

Kronosaurus was a kind of *plesiosaur*, alive during the *Mesozoic*. It was around 12 metres long and swam with four strong flippers.

LONG-NECKED LUNCH

Plesiosaurs were a long-necked marine reptile. Elasmosaurus was an extremely large type. Up to 14 metres long, half its length was neck.

Some people claim that a plesiosaur still lives in Loch Ness, Scotland.

OLD CROCS

Sarcosuchus was a river-dwelling ancestor of today's crocodile. At 13 metres long, it was big enough to prey on other dinosaurs as well as fish.

Record Breakers

The largest animals ever to exist on earth were alive during the Mesozoic period. So which were the biggest of these?

MIGHTY MEAT MUNCHER

Spinosaurus was the biggest ever meat-eating dinosaur, but it didn't feed on other dinosaurs. Its favourite food was fish.

TALL ORDER

At around 16 metres, Brachiosaurus could reach the leaves of tall trees while other sauropods had to feed at much lower levels.

LONG STRETCH

The record for the longest dinosaur ever discovered is held by Seismosaurus at an estimated 35 metres. Most of the length is neck and tail.

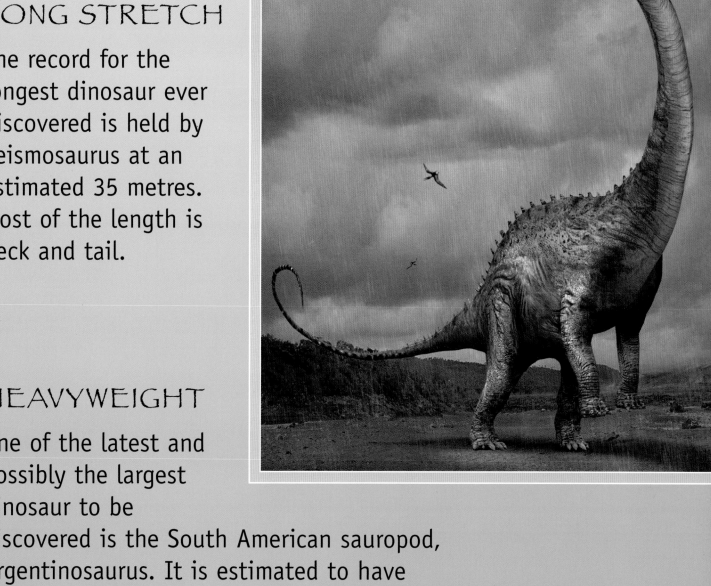

HEAVYWEIGHT

One of the latest and possibly the largest dinosaur to be discovered is the South American sauropod, Argentinosaurus. It is estimated to have weighed between 50 and 100 tonnes.

Glossary

Carnivore
Animal that eats other animals

Dinosaur
Ancient reptile with two or four legs which lived in the Mesozoic era

Fossil
Remains of a prehistoric plant or animal preserved in rock

Herbivore
Animal that feeds on plants

Mesozoic
The period between about 245 and 65 million years ago

Plesiosaur
Large reptile that swam in the sea in the Mesozoic era

Predator
An animal that catches, kills and eats other animals

Pterosaur
Flying reptile of the Jurassic period, with wings made of skin stretched over a long fourth finger

Reptile
Animal that lays eggs, usually has a smooth scaly skin, and is cold-blooded

Sauropod
Huge plant-eating dinosaur, usually with a long neck and massive legs

Further Reading

Dinosaur World Flying Giants
Ticktock Media, 2007

Mighty Giants
Michael Benton, Alligator Books
(Discovering Dinosaurs series), 2006

Dinosaurs
David Lambert, Dorling Kindersley
(Guide series), 2000

Dinosaurs
Stephanie Turnbull, Usborne
Publishing (Beginners series), 2006

Pop up Facts: Dinosaurs
Richard Dungworth, Templar
Publishing, 2006

Dinosaurs: The Most Complete, Up-to-Date Encyclopedia for Dinosaur Lovers of All Ages
Thomas R Holtz, Random House, 2007